OCTOPUS & SQUID

SEA MONSTERS

HOMER SEWARD

The Rourke Press, Inc.
Vero Beach, Florida 32964

PHOTO CREDITS
All photos © Marty Snyderman; except © Lynn M. Stone: page 13

EDITORIAL SERVICES:
Penworthy Learning Systems

Library of Congress Cataloging-in-Publication Data

Seward, Homer, 1942-
  Octopus and squid / Homer Seward.
    p. cm. — (Sea monsters)
  Includes index.
  Summary: Introduces the octopus and squid, their habits, physical appearance, and predators and prey.
  ISBN 1-57103-238-X
  1. Octopus—Juvenile literature. 2. Squids—Juvenile literature. [1. Octopus. 2. Squids.] I. Title II. Series: Seward, Homer, 1942- Sea monsters.
QL430.2.S48 1998
594'.56—dc21
                                              98–24059
                                                    CIP
                                                        AC

Printed in the USA

TABLE OF CONTENTS

Octopuses 5

Squids 6

Octopuses & Squids as Sea Monsters . . 8

The Giant Squid 11

What Octopuses & Squids Look Like . 12

Predator and Prey 14

Mollusks 17

Habits of Octopuses & Squids 18

Octopuses, Squids, and People 20

Glossary 23

Index 24

OCTOPUSES

The octopus is an amazing animal. It has no skeleton, but it is quite strong. It has no legs, but it has eight long arms.

Each octopus arm has one or two rows of small, cup-shaped suckers. They help the octopus get a grip on almost anything.

The octopus belongs to a large group of soft-bodied animals called **invertebrates** (in VER tuh brayts). They are not known for their brain power. But the octopus seems fairly smart, say **marine** (muh REEN) scientists.

Like its cousin the squid, the octopus is a creature of salt water.

An octopus catches prey and defends itself with eight sucker-lined arms and a parrot-like beak.

SQUIDS

Squids look much like octopuses. Soft and slippery, squids have eight short arms. Each arm has several suckers. Squids also have two fins.

Squids spend their lives in the open ocean. The fins help them steer as they swim. Sometimes squids swim with a great burst of speed.

Slippery squids are first cousins of octopuses. A squid's arms are much shorter for the squid's body length than octopus arms for the octopus.

Common squids mate over white, tube-shaped egg casings.

Unlike the octopus, a squid has a thin rod along its back for body support. Both squids and octopuses have two eyes and good vision.

OCTOPUSES & SQUIDS AS SEA MONSTERS

Books, movies, and old tales tell of frightful giant octopuses and squids. The real animals aren't nearly as big as the story animals. Nor are real octopuses and squids sea monsters. In fact, they are rarely a threat to people.

Octopuses can bite, however. They have hard, hooked jaws, like a parrot's beak.

The most dangerous octopus is the tiny blue-ringed octopus of Australia. Like a rattlesnake, it makes a deadly **venom** (VEN um), or poison. Its venom can kill a person.

You may not want to shake hands or arms with an octopus. More important, you don't want to be bitten by one!

THE GIANT SQUID

The giant squid is certainly not a sea monster. It's a huge, strange creature. Its two eyes are the size of soccer balls!

By size alone, the giant squid would be a scary animal to meet in the sea. A giant squid can weigh about 1,000 pounds (455 kilograms).

The huge squids probably aren't dangerous to people, but scientists know almost nothing about the way these animals behave. The giant squid is known only from dead ones that washed ashore.

Most squids, like this one, are far from giants, but they have the same oversized eyes for their body size.

WHAT OCTOPUSES & SQUIDS LOOK LIKE

Octopuses come in many sizes, from the size of thumbnails to lengths of 30 feet (9 meters). The biggest octopuses weigh about 600 pounds (about 270 kilograms).

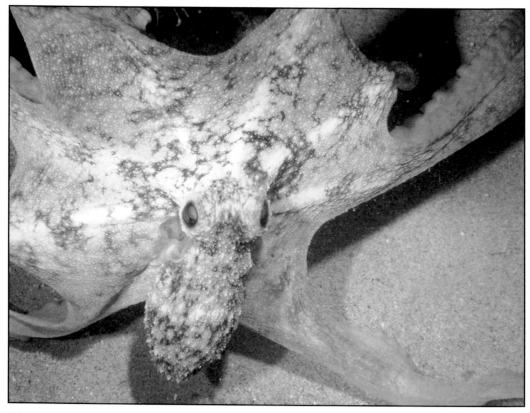

Octopuses come in many colors, and they can change colors.

Washed ashore by a storm in Florida, an octopus crawls out of its home in a clam shell.

The giant squid measures about 60 feet (18 meters). Its huge eyes are the largest of any known animal. Most squids are less than one foot (30 centimeters) long.

In addition to their arms, squids have two other "limbs," called tentacles. The tentacles grow from the squid's head and help catch **prey** (PRAY), the animals a squid eats.

PREDATOR AND PREY

Octopuses and squids live in oceans throughout the world. Octopuses like sea bottoms in both shallow and deep water. Both groups of animals are **predators** (PRED uh turz), or hunters.

Octopuses prey upon shrimp, crabs, and other marine animals. Octopuses use their arms to catch prey.

A squid hunts by snapping its tentacles forward, like long, stretchy hooks. The tentacles pull prey back to the eight waiting arms.

Both octopuses and squids are prey for larger ocean predators, including whales, sharks, and sea turtles.

While squids hunt the open seas, octopuses like to hide and wait for prey.

MOLLUSKS

Octopuses and squids belong to a group of boneless animals called **mollusks** (MAHL usks). Snails, oysters, clams, and mussels are also mollusks.

The giant squid is not only the largest mollusk but also the largest invertebrate in the world.

Mollusks have a hollow body space through which water passes. By squeezing water from this space, octopuses and squids can jet themselves quickly through the sea.

The closest mollusk cousins of octopuses and squids are the cuttlefish, chambered nautilus, and vampire squid.

Prized for its beautiful shell, the chambered nautilus is a close cousin of octopuses and squids.

HABITS OF OCTOPUSES & SQUIDS

Octopuses and squids are well known for their ability to release a cloud of "ink." The colored liquid helps hide their getaway. It may also confuse and scare a predator.

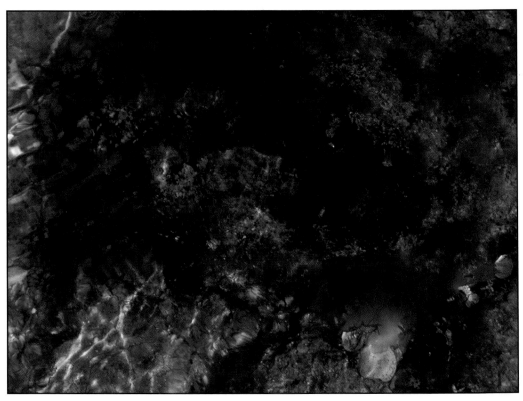

Squid and octopus "ink" helps an animal escape from its enemies.

An octopus can hide itself at home on the sea floor.

Octopuses are masters of **camouflage** (KAM uh flahj). They blend well with their surroundings. Octopuses and squids can change their color to match their surroundings. Some octopuses can even change the smoothness of their skin to match nearby objects.

OCTOPUSES, SQUIDS, AND PEOPLE

Many people fear the long, snaky arms of octopuses. The arms are usually harmless. Divers and fishermen know that an octopus bite is the real danger.

People catch octopuses and squids for food. Fried squid is sold as calamari (kal uh MAHR ee).

Scientists have used both octopuses and squids to study nerve endings. Their studies of these animals help them understand how human nerves work.

A diver shares the sea with giant Pacific octopus.

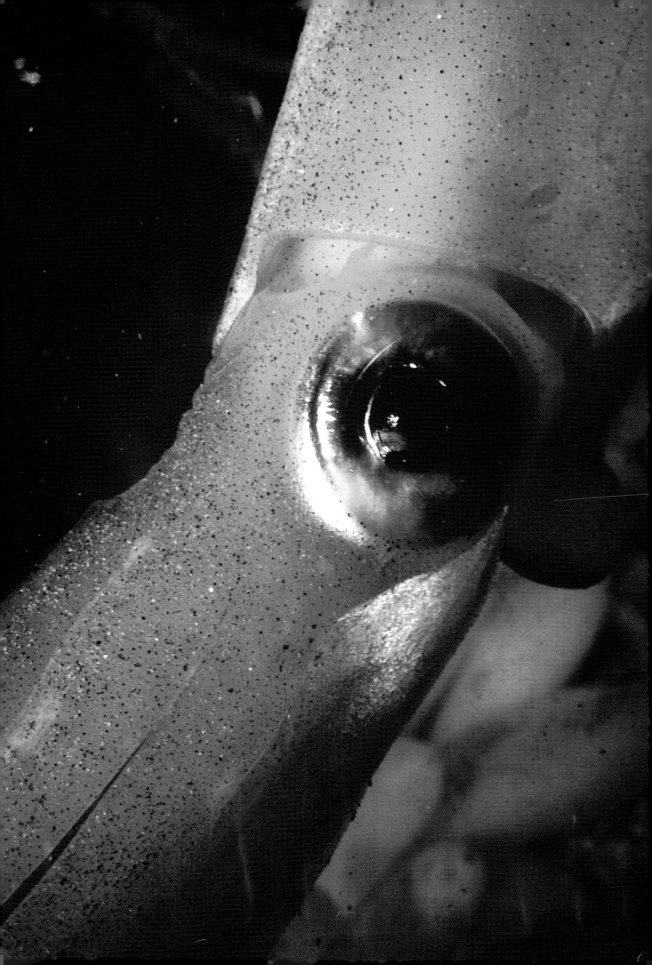

GLOSSARY

camouflage (KAM uh flahj) — the ability of an animal to use color, actions, and shape to blend into its surroundings

invertebrate (in VER tuh brayt) — an animal without a backbone; octopuses, squids, and other mollusks, for example

marine (muh REEN) — of or relating to the ocean

mollusk (MAHL usk) — simple, boneless animal including many with shells, such as oyster, clam, and snail

predator (PRED uh tur) — an animal that hunts other animals for food

prey (PRAY) — an animal that is hunted by another animal for food

venom (VEN um) — a poison produced by certain animals, including some octopuses

The squid's large eyes help it spot danger at a distance.

INDEX

arms   5, 6, 13, 20

calamari   20

camouflage   19

chambered nautilus   17

cuttlefish   17

eyes   7, 11, 13

fins   6

invertebrates   5, 17

jaws   8

mollusks   17

octopus   5, 7, 8, 12, 14,
   17, 18, 20

people   8, 20

prey   14

scientists   5, 11, 20

sea monsters   8

squid   6, 7, 8, 11, 13, 14,
   17, 18, 20

   giant   11, 13, 17

   vampire   17

suckers   5, 6

tentacles   13, 14

venom   8

FURTHER READING

Find out more about octopuses and squids with these helpful books:
Cerullo, Mary. *The Octopus.* Cobblehill, 1996.
Hunt, James. *Octopus and Squid.* Monterey Bay Aquarium, 1996.
Kite, Patricia. *Down in the Sea: The Octopus.* Whitman, 1993.
Martin, James. *Tentacles.* Crown, 1993.